CW00925788

Things
I Have
Noticed

Sophia Hembeck

first edition
published 2020, Edinburgh
- third print 2021 -

CONTENTS

intro

Intro

Most writers produce their memoirs a lot later in
life. After they have written their fiction, their
stories, they sail into their own life to examine. So in
many ways I'm doing this backwards. It's not
intentional. It just sort of happened. Like a hole in
a pipe it just started leaking. At first a soft dribble
that would find its way into my fiction. Thinking I
had it under control, not realising after a while that
the bucket I had put under it was overflowing and
flooding everything overnight.

This is all that was washed ashore. Those days.

These are the things I have noticed.

Things I Have Noticed

I don't want to tell you anything.
That's a lie.

Things I Have Noticed

part one: leaving

"The art of losing isn't hard to master;
so many things seem filled with the intent
to be lost that their loss is no disaster."

Elizabeth Bishop, One Art

1

I have left many things in my life. Hometowns,
first apartments, countries, bad relationships, older
versions of me, jobs, ideas, department stores,
theatre performances, conversations. Leaving is
what makes me thrive. My early twenties were full
of me leaving places and faces. But it all came to a
halt when I moved to Berlin. I had always thought it
to be the final destination. The epitome of cities.
Everyone I knew wanted to live there, was going to
live there or was already strutting down the wide
pavements with a new edgy haircut, dressed all in
black and possibly: a drug problem.[1]

---

[1] According to a questionnaire among Berlin students conducted by the
Charité 2019, in the following order of preference:
1. cannabis 2. MDMA/ecstasy, 3. amphetamine 4. cocaine

Things I Have Noticed

Berlin was the beginning and end, nothing to come after or to strive for. Anything past it would be downhill. – At least that's what I thought when I heaved my backpack and one suitcase up the stairs to my new apartment. Wooden floors, high ceilings, two balconies to be shared with three other women: I had been very lucky.

All I had with me was the backpack, a suitcase and a large sheep wool yoga mat. I had sold or given away all of my belongings from my previous home. This would be a fresh start, a clean slate.

The first week I cried in the evening over a recent break-up, listened to Lykke Li's album „I never learn", which was once interrupted by one of my new flatmates knocking on the door, asking me to turn it down because: She could hear the music in the bathroom next to it. My eyes rolled into my forehead after she left. In the morning I would ride my bike 10km to University, while occasionally being shouted at as „Move away cunt!".

– It was all very grand.

5 years later that bike would have fallen apart, the flatmate would have moved out, Lykke Li would be stuck way down in some playlist from 2014, my long hair cut and coloured many times. It would all seem like it had happened to someone else. Because I would have left this place, this person.

But for now I'm her again. That young 24-year-old trying to connect to a city she once declared: „Ugliest city I've ever been to." on a trip with her parents, ten years prior.

Things I Have Noticed

There's a lot of repair work that needs to be done.

I started by scraping the wall freeing it from its ugly wallpaper, hoping to find a greenish or reddish plaster, depending on how the old glue under the wallpaper had oxidized, as I had seen in other „artistic" flats. Naked walls were the thing. Like a currency for coolness. And if you were lucky, it looked so good, you barely had to hang up anything. It would just look great as it is.

Suffice to say: What I found under the first wall was a shit-brown. Someone apparently once had thought to scrape down the wallpaper, too and then decided that brown was the colour to cover it with. It must have been a very disturbed person, I cannot imagine otherwise.

„I'm not sure if that's okay." my new flatmate would say pointing at the blank walls, and I agreed „Why brown?" but she would not talk about that, she would mean the deposit and the contract – it's of course the annoying flatmate, the one who would move out a couple of months later, to live with her boyfriend, and thank god will then stop interrupting this re-cap and have no more say in this[2].

The naked walls were the most beautiful asset of the otherwise smallest room in the four-bedroom flat. I will look at them for one year and then move into the next bigger room with a balcony and then after another year move into the other similar-sized

---

[2] It was fine by the way.

room with a balcony next to it to then finally end up in the largest room, that has the size of a studio-flat where I will fit in a couch and a piano. Only to say goodbye to it all after one more year. I will grow into these walls and it will be hard to break me out of there.

But I will.

5 years later on a cold January morning I will book a little cottage to stay for four months in Edinburgh. And I will not return. I know this already as I'm pressing the button to charge my credit card a large amount of money, but I will tell no one. I'm too scared to tell them that I'm leaving for good.

Leaving is different every time. The first time I left, I was 16 and boarding a plane to Thailand. I cried so hard during the security check, that the staff member looking through my things overlooked the four lighters I had accidentally put into my carry-on bag. I had just started smoking. And apparently over the days of packing had kept putting all my lighters into the same bag. Not to forget.

Also with me a lot of shoes that I would never wear because it would be way too hot anyway and one pair of expensive wild-leather loafers that would be ruined by the monsoon rain a couple months later. None of these shoes would make it back to Germany.

I remember the shock/surprise/astonishment on peoples faces when I told them that I was going to live in Thailand for a year and I remember that feeling of smugness. I was a little smug then, I probably am still now. That feeling of: Yeah. I'm pretty exciting. Pretty bold. Pretty naive turned out to be more exact. I had no idea what was going to happen in Thailand. I opened the Thai language book for the first time on the plane.

– I was maybe a lunatic?

I was so sure of myself. So used to being understood. All of that would change during the 11 months I stayed somewhere in a 5 hour distance from Bangkok. Everything was always described in relation to Bangkok: places, people, looks, money. I was not prepared for it. Hence all the shoes. They would greet me in the morning when I would wear my white socks of the school uniform and slip smoothly into the black leather shoes, with the buckle strap, that made me feel like a schoolgirl from the 1950s. They would remind me, that once I had thought everyone would be able to speak English (wrong), there would be green hills covered in rice fields (wrong), I would not be homesick because I had never been in my life (very wrong).

I think about these Japanese rage rooms a lot.

2

We were told to write a letter to ourselves before we went. Something that would be waiting for us upon our return. I thought I would absolutely remember what was in that letter but it turned out, that after I had gotten back to Germany I would actually have forgotten even writing it. I was so surprised by my past-me's writing, urging me: Not to forget M.

My then boyfriend and first love. The reason why I had cried so heavily at the airport. Ironically he had been the one who had forgotten.

For a long time I had thought, that was what leaving does. Move your feet, lose your seat. There's no towel you can throw on a person. Reserving them for a later date.

It had hurt to read my past-self's wishes. My dreams and hopes. I remember sitting there in my yellow T-shirt, with the Thai monastery symbol stitched neatly on to it. Yellow the colour[3] of the King Bhumibol Adulyadej. It was the 60th anniversary of his ascent to the throne that year we lived in Thailand. Me and ten other german students. All scattered around Thailand in Thai host families. Some of them warm and welcoming, others less so.

I found myself thinking; if leaving everything behind you, your friends, your family, your language, your culture, had it been worth it?

~~Bankgog~~ ~~Bangkog~~ ~~Bankogk~~ Bangkok

15 years later I still don't know how to spell Bangkok. I don't know why I can never remember where the g goes, before the k, or how many k's? *Groong taip* that's how Thai people call it. Phonetically written *Krung Thep*. But it's a G not a K. It's *goa gai*. G for chicken. *Gai* meaning chicken. Phonetically written *koo kai*. Meaning little chicken. Like the clothing brand KOOKAI, I kept thinking when I first learned the Thai alphabet.   Like a secret code only I – now a student of the Thai

---

[3] In Thailand, it is widely believed that dressing in a certain colour each day will bring you good luck. The code is: Monday, yellow; Tuesday, pink; Wednesday, green; Thursday, orange; Friday, blue; Saturday, purple; Sunday, red. Black is reserved for funeral days. The King was born on a Monday, that's why his colour is yellow.

language – could decode. Sometimes I tried to tell people about it, but the audience usually just shrugged in apathy and said: „So why were you in Thailand?“

I never understood why the phonetic alphabet, translating the Thai alphabet deferred so far from the actual sounds that I was hearing. It seemed a bit like a conspiracy against *Farangs,* a word I was introduced to mean „western people“ which I later found out usually just meant „white people“. They all came with their hard K's trying to say chicken / *gai* because their books told them so. Bewildered that nobody understood.

When you connect to a place, lived there, formed memories of soups transported in little translucent plastic bags and hot metal engines that could and would burn your calves when you're sitting upon a motorbike with two other girls, you keep looking for it even when you're long gone. The minute it pops up it seems like a specific message directed at you. When I heard 2016 that the King had died I felt a strange pang of sorrow. I went on Facebook to look at what my old Thai school friends were posting. Liking some posts, clicking through images. Some of them had married already and children of their own, some of them had ventured outside Thailand as au pairs and students. I looked at their lives, almost like a stranger stalking random people on the internet and only when I dug deeper, I saw that for a brief moment, I had been among them. We had been friends.

„Do you want to be my friend Fasai?" a little note with a smiley and hearts drawn on it, was passed to me during French lessons. I had picked French, even though I was not able to speak any but I figured, why learn just one language, when you can learn two?[4]

During the first weeks I had received a lot of these sweet notes, making me feel welcomed. They had also offered me a couple of nicknames. As all Thai people have a nickname. And I had paid extra attention to not choose *Moo*, meaning pig. One of the alumni exchange students that had spoken to us during the preparation week, had been called *Moo* by his friends, not knowing for a long time, what it actually meant. Then I still wasn't sure, whether I was even going to be in Thailand choosing nicknames, because they still had not told me, if I was going to get the full scholarship which I needed.

We were also told during that week: People touching our skin, touching our hair, wanting to take photographs, was likely to happen. One girl once actually had a fan club at her school, one of the advisors told us, a sparkle in her eye, clearly the grand prize. I was determined for that. I wanted a fan club. She was very pretty, the advisor had added. Needless to say I was craving that validation. No fan club, no pretty.

„I want to be like chocolate." I will tell my therapist some years later, when we talk about my

---

[4] I did not learn French that year.

need to be liked by ... well ... everyone. And she will stare at me and give me a very rare half-smile[5] that said „You can't possibly be serious" and say something smart like „Why do you want to be something that is consumed by everyone?"

My host sister Melon was obsessed with her face. It was before the whole selfie cult took over. It was before the word "selfie" was even invented. Before I had my Facebook account which I only created to keep in touch with my Thai friends. For a couple of years it was my little internet bubble that connected me to them.

Nowadays of course: Facebook is dead[6]. In a way social media always has been. We're dragging it with us like a dead corpse we can't shake off our backs. We learned to dance with it. I remember my own pre-smartphone phase and my annoyance at my then boyfriend who's first action in the morning was to check his phone and scroll through his feed. Of course this morning like every other morning I do the same. I convince myself that if I were in a partnership I would refrain from it. I would have better things to do than check my emails, messages and in my case Instagram-stories. But evidence of other people's complaints about their spouses highlights the fact that: We're all dancing with the dead. Our polished, flat, 2-D versions of ourselves.

---

[5] Usually she refrained from facial expressions.

[6] Of course Facebook is also owning Instagram and other platforms so in fact it is still very alive. But I kind of wish it wasn't.

Melon was an early-adapter. Melon had a blackberry with an internet connection and front camera (very important), as I had inherited her flipphone that was able to shoot shitty images, that made everyone look like a Zelda character.

They were a very generous family. They were also very wealthy. The gap between wealthy and poor in Thailand is vast. When I was there in 2006 some of the villages still didn't have electricity. That's what I would always read in the books and preparation sheets we got beforehand. Because electricity in the western world is vital, where are we going to plug in the computer? What's the wifi password?

I used the word wealthy earlier because I don't think these people were necessarily rich. They only had money.

I don't want to romanticise poverty in Thailand, I don't think poor people in Thailand are necessarily happier and I think the distribution of wealth, the inherent hierarchy and rights of workers need much improvement. It's just whether you can afford an air-conditioning or a big house where everyone has their own room, a western toilet or warm water for your shower; it is worth questioning if it's really enhancing one's own quality of living significantly. Or if being able to nap throughout the day when you feel like it and enjoy a nice meal and a good chat with your neighbors and relatives who show up regularly during the day might not be a whole lot worth as well. This view of pity is what I'm defying.

What is really important in life? Can it be measured by the world bank?

There's a TED Talk I watched recently by a Thai man called Jon Jandai: "When I was a kid everything was fun and easy, but when the TV came, many people came to the village, they said: 'You are poor. You need to chase success in your life. You need to go to Bangkok to pursue success.' So I felt bad. I felt poor." He speaks then about his experience working in Bangkok: at least eight hours a day. Barely having enough money to pay for rent and food. He started to question his motives: „When I work so hard, why is my life so hard? (…) I started to think about, why did I have to be in Bangkok?" He comes to the conclusion that back at his village, his childhood: life was good. It was fun. He is holding the TED talk in English. But I'm sure what he is talking about here is: สนุก / *sanook*.

สนุก / *sanook* is one of the most important words in Thai language. The essence of why anything really should be done. It means: fun/to have a good time/to enjoy oneself/to derive pleasure and joy from something. If it's not สนุก / *sanook* it shouldn't be done. It's an ethos. A way of living your life. It means that life needs to be enjoyable, focusing on the process, being in the moment. It's not a team-building measure, a break from work, a holiday. It just is. Integrated every day. It's the answer to your: why?

So Jandai realises he did not have any **สนุก** / *sanook* anymore, and decides to go back to where he once felt it. He leaves Bangkok and his work behind to start a new life back home in his village. Focusing on the things he essentially needs: food, water and a roof over his head. He starts to sow rice and plant a little garden. Everyday he only works two hours, sowing seeds, working on the field. For the rest he enjoys himself: **สนุก** / *sanook*. Bit by bit he is producing enough rice and vegetables not just for his family to eat but to sell some on the market.

"Before I thought that stupid people like me who never got a good grade at school, cannot have a house. Because people who are cleverer than me (…) they get a job but they need to work more than 30 years to have a house. (…) But then I started to do earthly building[7], it's so easy[8]."

Every day he works on his cob house for just two hours. Three months later his house is finished. "And another friend who's the most clever (…) he spent three months to build his house, too. But he

---

[7] I think some of his genius is lost in translation in this talk. He actually started to build houses with cob in 1997, which is a very sustainable way of building a house, by using only natural resources.

[8] Obviously less restrictions on building houses and climate make it a lot easier to build a house in Thailand. But I think his message is still valid.

has to be in debt. He has to pay for his debt for 30 years."

สนุก / *sanook mai*? They would ask me, all the time. Is it fun? Are you enjoying yourself? And I usually would reply: สนุก / *sanook maak*. Yes, a lot of fun. I never really thought about answering anything else.

Learning a new language is like studying someone else's thought pattern. I had done it through music. Karaoke to be specific. My host family had a Karaoke room which technically was just the room where the big TV lived. All bedrooms had TVs but this one was a flatscreen that was so big you had to step back a couple of meters, to actually get the whole picture. I would spend hours alone in that room, singing along to *Bodyslam*. My then favourite Thai rock band. Googling them it turns out they are still a band. I'm kind of glad. Good for them. I remember they were my host brothers favourite band and my first concert in Thailand. I can still see the blue smoke and the more or less empty dance floor that night in the only big club in Surin. The audience mingling in the back as if too shy to be seen by the band. I remember my host father being very uneasy and us leaving in the middle of their act. „It's getting dangerous." my host brother whispered and I didn't really understand why. I guessed then what he meant was, that people were getting drunk.

Most of us did not learn Thai that year. The ones that lived in very touristic areas would mostly speak English. Nobody expecting them to learn Thai. „Can you be my English teacher?" was a frequently asked question, which always made me a bit sad. I really wanted to learn Thai.

„So why Thailand?" people still ask me that. When they do, they point towards my tattoo that was inked on my left wrist two years after my exchange year. By a Thai guy on Ko Phi Phi, who without my interference would have spelled it wrong.

After finishing high school I had gone back for a holiday. Me and my Mum. Four weeks just me and her, backpacking through Thailand. The Thailand I had experienced so thoroughly, I wanted to show her everything. Bangkok with it's delicious street food markets, Tuk Tuks, Chiang Mai and the temple Wat Doi Suthep where you can shake a bamboo stick with a number on, out of a box and then go to a drawer with that number and get a piece of paper where your fortune is written on (my favourite part), endless Thai massages, my old school, my Thai host family, the place where I had had a motorbike accident, the elephants in the reservoir, the food market where I always had gotten *boa bia* (Thai spring rolls) that were always finished before I got home, the beach where I had gotten majorly drunk on several buckets (actual buckets) of Mai Thai or Stormy or Sex on the Beach pronounced Sex on the Bisch, which always sounded a bit wrong, but very funny when you were drunk.

It was the first and since then only trip me and my Mum ever took together. It was also the first time I saw my Mum out of her normal habitat which consisted then of our house, me and my older sister who still lived with us, my Dad, our small town, where she was born and which she had never left, house chores and once or twice a day giving a pilates or aerobic class. I guess we all have to grow up eventually. For me: Thailand would mark the starting point of that.

Things I Have Noticed

There we were.
Lying next to all the things we could have been.

3

Most people think their childhood was happy till they sit down in a room with abstract art on the wall in front of them a clipboard and behind that clipboard a person with a blank expression. At least that's how it was for me.
Leaving as it turns out had been a constant pattern in my formative years. Long before I stepped on that plane and left. – People had left me.
During my childhood and early adolescence we had been a foster family for temporary cases meaning: children who usually had parents that were – due to various reasons – unable to care for them for a while would stay with us. A while could take 24h to a year. A while could sometimes mean forever.

Mostly they would stay with me, because I had the biggest room. Some days I would come home from school and someone new would sit at our table. They would be shown to my room, to the second bed that was waiting for them, diagonally opposite mine. At night I would look up and see them sleeping there. And later I would look up and sometimes miss them.

I would not miss all of them. Because some of them had used all my precious Pocahontas stationery that I had gotten for my Birthday to write to their Mothers.

„And it was not replaced?" my therapist would ask years later. Which is the exact moment I realised that all this time I had been telling myself a different story. A story of a happy foster family that was always welcoming and warm, where everyone was seen and needs were met. It crumbled right before me. Because how I used to tell this story was this: It is always very exciting to have someone new in the family. Not knowing if one or two new children will suddenly wait for you at home, a room, it's challenging but usually we get along very well. One of the girls turned out to be my best friend during primary school. I like having new temporary siblings. I like having a lot of people in the family. Sure we were already six people, but the more the merrier right? It was always a new adventure and I learned a lot about sharing and caring for other people.

This is what I told the local newspaper journalist that once came to our house, because he was writing an article about our experience as a foster family. We had recently stopped being one due to the fact that my brother had moved out, my sister was doing an au pair in the US and me and my other sister now full teenagers: the wholesome family structure was quite off. While my sister rolled her eyes and occasionally said contradicting things to the journalist, about our parents not having enough time for us sometimes and that some of the children had been quite antisocial, all of which I would sweep to the side with a broad smile. Nothing had been bad, everything had been fine, my parents had always made the best choices, we were all very very happy and on board with it.

Years later immediately after that therapy session I would call my sister on the phone and we would finally have an earnest conversation of what actually had happened.

"Why can I not sleep in the free room next to Melon's?" I'm a bit upset but I try not to show it (too much.) Which is not working as well as I'd like to think. My eyes are clenching intensely. "In Thailand sisters usually sleep together, in some families even the whole family sleeps together in one room. So you'll not be lonely[9]" Is what my advisor says as I am trying to tell her, that as a

---

[9] Sleeping next to someone that doesn't speak to you is probably the loneliest I've ever been.

sixteen year old, I find it a bit weird[10] not to have my own room, let alone my own bed. But she just shrugs her shoulders. "The room next to Melon's is your host brothers. I hear that he is not sleeping there, but it's where he stores his clothes. So."

Ironically I am living with one of the wealthiest families in the whole province, yet there isn't another room for me. There is another house, but ghosts[11] are living there. At least that is what I am told. My host mother, that I call Mae, has seen one. A bad one. Just as the house was finished building. She might have been joking, she might have been lying, she also might actually believe that there was a ghost haunting the new place, the result is the same: They are not going to move there, they will stay in the old one. Which isn't exactly old, anyway. It just has an enormous amount of open hall space and quite small rooms on one side. I have no idea who the architect is, but that person apparently likes to cycle indoors or whatever they were thinking why anyone would need that much hall space. Maybe they are a squash player.

My Dad used to play squash. It used to be a total thing. Where's Dad? He's playing squash. For a while I didn't know what squash was, so I made up my own thing. Squash was where Dads go on a

---

[10] Very very weird. Not to mention the amount of stuffed animals that were lined up in the shelves!

[11] Ghosts are a total thing in Thailand. They even have their own small versions of houses in front of the actual houses. And get offered food. It's quite beautiful.

29

weekly basis, it involved a squash partner and it was a very serious endeavor. In my head it looked something like a giant ball pit for grown-ups as I had seen at IKEA, where you would get squashed by the balls. I was quite disappointed when I found out, that it's two sweaty men in a room, hitting a tennis ball against a wall.

"Isn't it boring?" I would ask him, after I had found out. And he was a bit offended I guess. Like Dads get when questioned in their lifestyle choices. Pretty soon after that he stopped playing and we never talked about it again, though I don't think there's a correlation. Where's Dad? In the basement.

My first host Dad[12] in Thailand had no name or at least not that I remember ever addressing him. He would have been *Khun Poa* but again no memory of ever using that word. He was rarely with us and if he was, he was mostly quiet. A feature he shared with my actual Dad. The only time he ever really spoke to me was when he shouted at me across the table in a restaurant we frequently visited.

I had asked to go on the school trip to Chiang Mai with my classmates instead of going with Melon who was two years younger and at that point already mostly not speaking to me. The whole school was going but there were separate trips planned. One for the students who were poor and only able to afford cheap travel and

---

[12] Which, yes, means there will be a second host dad.

accommodation in the temple and one for the wealthy students that slept in a hotel with a private mini bus. I wanted to sleep in the temple with my friends. Which had caused a major conflict.

I was about to make them lose their face. Why did the *farang* not want to join her host sister? Why did she want to sleep with hundreds of other students in the temple, with three showers to share? Were they not paying for her? – From their perspective: I made no sense.

Image is very important in Thailand. Beauty. Appearance. There is an important word called *kreng jai* which literally means in awe of the heart. It's deeply linked to the idea that one must save their own and other people's faces. That they must not lose it. Open confrontation, criticizing anyone, pointing out mistakes all of it is avoided at any cost. To the extend that when I had accidentally worn Melon's skirt to school and it being a lot shorter on me, due to my height – I was constantly two heads taller than everybody else – my advisor Miss Polly had called me to her office and then made up this whole story about another exchange student, who had dared to shorten her skirt and how everyone had been disappointed to see it. It was quite Shakespearesque. Like Hamlet, when he's putting on a play where a King is murdered to reveal the actual murder of his father by his uncle. I had cried that day in her office, obviously not caring to lose my face.

I'm sorry. I didn't know.

„It's okay that you cry now" she had said. „But don't do it again." And I wasn't sure if she had meant the skirt or the crying.

Possibly it was when I pretended to faint that I had hit the lowest point of my re-enactment of 19th century hysteria. I wanted to change host families. It had been on my mind a lot in the past months as the tension between me and Melon had caused me to eat less, not so secretly smoke in the shower and sleep most of the school hours in the nurse's office. The beds had been installed for children who were having a headache, tummy ache or something similar non-life-threatening, waiting for school to end. The minute I realised that I could literally just go there to sleep, because I was so tired from the late dinners and Melon watching Korean soap operas on TV all night, it was my sanctuary for a while. I had been severely depressed but no one told me.

Interestingly I was mostly aware of my questionable methods to get attention for my distress, albeit not able to prevent any of them. I guess what I actually was trying to do, was get attention from myself.

Just after my 17th birthday and 7 months after arriving in Bangkok I decided for the last 3 months I wanted to leave my current host family. I had known it for a long time but like most situations that are not exactly bad enough – bad but one could imagine worse – they are the hardest to leave behind. Because it might not get better and it could definitely get worse. The morning I woke up at my friends house before Christmas, the first time I was ever allowed to sleep over at another person's house, it suddenly became light and easy: I wanted to stay with her. With her family. In her house. In the countryside. With a little market to walk to and a motor roller to drive around and trips to Ko Samet, a small island close to Bangkok and other parts of Thailand.

I had lived in a climatized emotional and actual icebox. I needed to leave again.

I never found out exactly why Melon stopped speaking to me. Over the years I have accumulated various reasons that all somewhat evolved around the fact, that I probably did everything very wrong in her perspective. She also wasn't a very talkative person to begin with, but there's a difference in someone being quiet like my Dad and someone not answering after the fifth time of you asking them a question. Which is why I was very surprised that Melon was actually mad at me for leaving.

So mad that she even took my phone. Her old phone. Image was very important to Melon. As she is unthreading the stitches of my blouse with a small knife, erasing the last name we have shared for seven months, a mark of her rage will always be visible above my chest. The little dots where the needle once has pulled the blue thread through, now empty.

Her father later ordered her to give the phone back to me, a gesture that made me reconcile with him.

Thanks Poa.

In a manner of *kreng jai* / saving face I had told my host family that I simply wanted to experience a different side of Thailand (which was true) and that it had nothing to do with them (complete lie, that we all knew it was but pretended not to know) and that I just wanted to live with my best friend (very true). I still wonder sometimes what actually had happened, why it had gotten so hard and complicated with my first host family. Everything had started so promising. I still remember waking up the first morning, on my side of the bed a little note written by Melon: Good morning Sophia. I hope you have a wonderful day!

Mai bpen rai Melon's grandfather would say. Not her actual grandfather as I found out much, much later but a well-spoken english scholar, former journalist and retired teacher, that they had asked to accompany them, when they were picking me up in Bangkok and who was occasionally around or on the phone to translate things. Though when I met him the first time, I just thought he was family. A common mistake amongst foreigners, because everyone in Thailand is an aunt, an uncle, brother or sister and so on.

Mai bpen rai is probably the most used phrase in Thai and means: It doesn't matter / Don't worry. It's supposed to be soothing and a relief, that things are always changing and nothing ever is constant.
Melon's grandfather would often talk about buddhism and its lectures. How one must feel nothing. And love the empty water glass. I don't remember exactly how that story went, it involved a glass of water and someone being thirsty, it was meant as a parable to suffering and content. I just know that it often caused me to despair because I was trying to tell him that I was sad and lonely and didn't understand why Melon was not talking to me any longer and then he would start talking about that glass of water again.

I'm bored. *Chan bua.* I used to say it all the time at my old host family's house. Walking around from the Karaoke room to the office, to the kitchen, back to the Karaoke room. I would talk to the three maids who usually were working in the kitchen, but once the family found out about it, they raised their concerns and sent me to the Karaoke room again.

It was weird to live in a house where there were maids. At first it was thrilling to tell everyone at home, how I was living with a very wealthy family. How they had bought me clothes and were giving me pocket money and a phone and an expensive wrist watch, two actually. How they were building a private golf course, for the western investors, when they'd come by for a meeting. It was something to

35

talk about, a surprise, like, ha tricked you: I'm actually living with the upper class now.

What I would leave out for a while was: I was not able to walk anywhere by myself, not allowed to mingle with anyone they didn't approve and most of the gifts that I had gotten, I was not allowed to choose them which left me with a lot of stuff I didn't even care to take home with me.

I lived the whole cliche of rich-girl-golden-cage. Interestingly I always had thought I'd be able to pull that off. Obeying rules, being homely like an Enid Blyton[13] character. To do as I'm told, be home by six and keep my school uniform nice and neat. I even cut my hair below my earlobes because the school rules demanded it so. I didn't actually have to do it, as one of my teachers pointed out: „You're a *farang*. You look different anyway."
But I wanted to. I wanted to fit in and to please. The only problem was: It was just so boring.

Nobody had told me how boring it was to follow the rules. At home I rarely had to follow rules, not because there were none but because rules are only really rules, when you acknowledge them in the first place. When rules make sense to you, they usually don't feel like it at all. I had thought I could be home by six, which as a sixteen year old who was

---

[13] Think of "The Twins at St.Clare's" (sidenote: "German girls loved Hanni and Nanni. The six-book series was really popular in Germany, where Patricia and Isobel became Hanni und Nanni and readers received bonus hair bobbins." https://www.dailyedge.ie/enid-blyton-st-clares-facts-628551-Oct2012/) I loved Hanni & Nanni

turning seventeen who already drank, smoked and had sex was: infantilising. What I couldn't even fathom was that I might not be able to leave the house after school at all.

In a way I always knew that I was going to leave. I was just waiting for the right timing. When I stayed at my friends house, which I had only been allowed to sleep at due to some obscure scheme by my advisor who had told my host family a straight lie, about some english teacher convention in a nearby province, so I could be there. Looking outside her window, the air floating freely into the room, the heat, the smells of cooked food: I could touch freedom.

The great thing about getting older is that songs turn out to be little time capsules, they catapult you right back to your 15th birthday.
Kissing that boy you've been crushing on for two years.

4

There's no better feeling than waking up in a bed by yourself, when you've just left someone who really didn't belong in your life any longer. That feeling when you stretch your arms out and that someone is not there to tell you to: Lower your chin, because it makes you look arrogant. Or is questioning every word you say about what had happened the other night, when you went out with your friends. That moment of freedom is priceless. I like to condense it, freeze it and store it in every corner of my brain, for when that moment comes, when that freedom feels more like a chore, a destiny I didn't choose, I can remind myself that at least, at least we have left that terrible situation.

That is the good kind of leaving. I have experienced and seen it over the years many times: friends suddenly thriving when that dead weight of a partner finally was dropped. That endless analysis of their character of why they were doing the things they were doing, with the ultimate conclusion: That. They. Just. Sucked.

I love that kind of leaving. It's like a super power. Because everything is better once you leave. Obviously not forever, obviously there are reasons why one was in that situation in the first place and taking a good look at yourself to find out why, is a mandatory step that should not be forgotten. But relationships that end with a bang of relief, usually punch you that hard in the face, that most learnings are quite visible.

„All writing is revenge", said the cuban poet Reinaldo Arenas. Which for a good portion is probably true. But not all writing is revenge. Some of it is a love letter. Because sometimes you leave, when you don't want to. Sometimes you have to leave.

After I got back from Thailand everything had changed. It was March and I was freezing. I had no clothes to wear, the dresses and skirts I had brought from Thailand in pink and pastel colours belonged to another version of myself that was starting to clash with my past-punk-self. I also had no boyfriend. Before Thailand I would wear chucks and put buttons on my schoolbag. I had worn bright red hair and a wonky asymmetric haircut I had given myself in a moment of boredom. Since then that colour had been washed out and dyed over with a dark brown and a nice shoulder length bob. I had at least 10 items with Hello Kitty on them.

Looking in the mirror next to our front door, wearing a thick black parker and under it a pink t-shirt and denim jeans that had flowers stitched on them, waiting for my not yet ex-boyfriend: I had an identity crisis. Everyone had always been preparing us for going abroad and the culture shock we'd for sure encounter. Coming back had never been something I had given much thought.

I was freezing in my parker as we took a walk to the bench, our bench in the nearby forest. The one where we had sat two years before on our first date and me exaggerating my life story a bit. I wanted to impress him so much, wanted him to like me so much, that in retrospect I definitely overdid it. He said: I love you, three weeks later and I would be angry and question his feelings that after three weeks only he would use these words. How dare he love me, just like that. In fact I was scared. It scared me so much, that I forbid him to say it again for a while.

There were many things during that year that broke our relationship apart. There was no Skype or WhatsApp yet. There were very expensive phone calls from debit cards and emails. There was the day I had a motorbike accident and my heart broken afterward.

There was another girl.
It had all been too much and not enough.
And there he was, sitting on that bench, asking me
again and again: „Why did you leave me? Why did
you go to Thailand?"

The easy answer was. I had watched a movie.
Anna and the King. A film which paradoxically is
banned in Thailand. I had seen it a couple of weeks
before my interview with the exchange committee
and fallen in love with the architecture, the colours,
the landscape, the beauty of Thai women and their
dresses.

Initially I had put India as my first choice and
then – impulsively during the interview – changed it
to Thailand. There was one full scholarship for
each country: Thailand. India. China. Japan. That
was the order of my preference.

The more complex answer is: I just felt like it.
Something drew me to do it. It was an adventure, I
just couldn't say no to. It's hard to explain to
someone who does not want to go to Thailand
when they're fifteen years old but to me it just
sounded like the best idea ever.

It sounded like something that I would do. I
guess that's the thing about life choices. When they
have our name written on them, we simply cannot
refuse.

– I do sometimes think about what would have
happened if I had stayed. And there was once or

twice a moment where I regretted my decision, as it had caused some people a lot of pain, including myself. But what I regret today is not leaving to pursue something that was important for myself. To love is to cause each other pain. It's inevitable. The only thing that I regret is: I wish I had loved more.

Things I Have Noticed

I think about a line in Gilmore Girls a lot: „I want you to be dancing through the woods, crazy happy"
I remind myself from time to time. Like I'm my own mother.

5

The day I left therapy, I had a panic attack at Netto, a german supermarket, which of all supermarkets, probably is the worst one to have a panic attack. A Netto is usually crammed with products, customers, narrow aisles and the employees seem to be on a race to get your groceries through the scanners as quickly as possible. Netto is the high-pressure cooker of supermarkets. You don't want to be in one, when you're losing your grip on reality.

Since I had started therapy, I had talked about ending it. Somewhere in between I had stopped and actually accepted my fate but as the year was nearing an end, leaving was on my mind again:

Therapy was just so fucking hard.

I didn't like it. I didn't like to tell a complete stranger my problems, I didn't like that stranger to assess my mental health, I didn't want to be the object of someone else's analysis.

And quite frankly: I was afraid that I wasn't just having a millennial quarter-life-crisis #depression #anxiety. I was afraid that I was so far off the shore, that I would not ever be able to swim back. I was afraid that I would drown.

Sometimes you find strengths from a younger self. A couple of years before the day I left therapy I had been on a night train to Zurich to visit my then boyfriend. It was his graduation ceremony the next day, after studying for 5 long years to get a master degree in history - it was quite a big thing. I wanted to be there, celebrate with him. Our relationship had been: toxic[14].

He had behaved badly. I had behaved badly. We were making each other quite miserable, but were not able to break it off just yet. I was waiting for a sign. Not from the outside, because they were plenty. They were waving at me frantically: Hello? Helloooo? We are here? Acknowledge us!

I ignored them like ghosts. They were invisible to me. I was waiting for a sign from the inside. A specific feeling: The knowing. I had felt it on that bench. I was waiting to feel it now.

Sleeping on a night train by myself was never a thing that I considered particularly dangerous.

---

[14]As many articles that I read during that time confirmed.

49

Usually there were other passengers nearby and also where would you go to escape? There's also something cosy and secure about the single compartments on these types of trains. You close the door, switch off the lights, you signify to everyone else: Don't come in here. This is my house. No trespassing.

I love long train journeys. For once you're still and the world is enfolding next to you. It centers me. I usually have a book with me that I never open, because listening to music and just staring at whatever is happening outside of my window is enough.

I am enough.

Night trains also have that extra feeling of nostalgia. Arriving by night train is practically like arriving from another century, where women still wear hats and curl their hair and carry small leather suitcases with all their belongings in and men keep handkerchiefs for them in their pockets. „I didn't know they still exist!" People would frequently say and then fall into a sort of nostalgic moment themselves of their journeys through Europe in the 80s, when I told them about how I got to my current destination.

– It's funny how you never know exactly how you will react when faced with danger. You might lie in bed at night, alone in your flat and imagine a burglar coming in and locate your first weapon readily in your mind (the candle holder next to your bed or the ceramic plant pot) but you never know if you'd jump up immediately and be able to make a call to the police while your hiding in the safest spot (behind the curtains, because that's actually a really good hiding place, a burglar would probably not look behind them, whereas under the bed is way too obvious and they're probably going to look in the wardrobe. So. Anyway.) Or whether you'll freeze under your covers, pretending to sleep. You just don't know till it happens.

I had put my bag under my head and all my valuable belongings: wallet & phone into the pockets of my jeans. I wasn't really worried about someone trying to rob me but just to be safe. To get some sleep and not wonder where my stuff was.

The next thing I remember is a shadow hovering above me.

WHAT ARE YOU DOING HERE?!

Someone was screaming with a strange deep voice. That someone was me. My arm shooting to the left, defending me as if my body was functioning all by itself. I turned on the light and a man in his mid-thirties was looking at me wide eyed: terrified.

As he should have been because it turned out that, when faced with danger. I would go in for the kill.

After a quick interrogation and me analysing the situation.

> *Who are you?*
> *Which stop are we at?*
> *Where is your luggage?*
> *When did you get on the train?*

And a lot of:

> *You scared me.*
> *Why did you sneak up on me?*

He simply left. I don't know where he went or what he actually had intended to do by walking into a dark compartment and hovering above a woman who was sleeping, but it actually didn't matter to me. Because I had found out something about myself, as I sat down again and looked out into the black night. Something I had forgotten in the past four years of my relationship with my then boyfriend: I could actually rely on myself.

That moment flared up again as I was walking down the steps from my therapist office. It had been weird and strange and very very scary to tell her: This will be our last session. From now on I will cope by myself.

We had been talking about the end of therapy for several sessions now in the past weeks and I had realised that it was time. Like when you're at a party and you suddenly acknowledge that almost everyone already left and it dawns on you, that if you don't want to be the last person to go, it really is time to pack up your things and get going.

I had gotten up from my chair, said my goodbyes and was ready to leave, the door handle in one hand, sort of waiting for the host, in this case my therapist to say some final words and wish me well.

She didn't. She just sat there and reluctantly gave me the piece of paper to sign my ending to therapy. She would say: How I was showing ambivalence towards my decision and I would say: Hand me the piece of paper.

I don't know if that is how you end therapy. If it always feels like, almost violently ripping yourself away from it.

I guess it is different when you actually choose therapy. When you really seek it and are ready for it. Because the reason why I had gone to therapy, would practically leave me no choice. The reason why I would leave Berlin.

Every time I see "fragile" written on a parcel, I think:
Me, too.

Things I Have Noticed

Things I Have Noticed

part two: searching

"I am out with lanterns, looking for myself."

Emily Dickinson

1

I sometimes wonder what it feels like to have a writer in the family. As I am the writer in my family[15] I certainly have a blindspot. I don't know what it feels like to be written about. Which is not exactly true. I have writer friends and the occasional quote or situation I was part of has mingled itself into their writing but I don't think it's the same. Family is different. We all are maybe not our truest selves within our family context but surely our most consistent. As if the moment we walk over that threshold of „home home" we are transformed to whatever version we were at age thirteen.

Me: loud, lazy, always in a fight with my sister. Changing your behaviour around family is like trying to fit a square through a hole. You will have to take off the edges, to make it work. And that will hurt.

---

[15] So far.

This is going to be a tough one. Searching does that to you. Searching for love, approval, assurance, safety, adventure, truth. When you're searching for something you're always a bit lost. You're unsure of yourself, the path, the thing that you're looking for. There's a lack of something, an equation to solve, a balance to retrieve again. We're howling into the night hoping for answers, hoping that it's not just an echo of ourselves. The year I turned 25 I found myself howling a lot.

Berlin started how Thailand had ended. With a breakup. After that moment on the night train, I had remembered something about myself, that I couldn't deny any longer: I was actually able to take care of myself. – It's also quite telling when your first gut reaction to: "Do you want me to accompany you to the interview at the University of Arts?" Is a searing: "no!"

Either way I was alone when I arrived on a cold morning at the beginning of February, in front of me the majestic white columns that I hoped to walk through for the next four years. I didn't know anyone. All I knew was, that this was something I had been working for, for a long time.

I had prepared myself by watching a lot of interviews with the actress Jennifer Lawrence, trying to emulate that perfect balance of raw honesty, charme and relatability. – In retrospect: I might have overdone it[16]. I think there was a moment

---

[16] Again.

when I asked them to: Just let all twelve contestants be in the new class[17]. But somehow I got in. Jennifer Lawrence or not.

Szenisches Schreiben which means "scenic writing", I assure you the name makes as much sense in German as in English (not a lot), is the only writing course in Germany that focuses solely on playwriting. Every two years there are about 300-500 people applying to get in. Being one of the few who were chosen, felt like it's own accomplishment. I swore to never miss a class or homework: I would be diligent, meticulous, inventive. I would not tire or ever forget my huge privilege to be there. Around three weeks later, I think, I must have forgotten all about it though.

In the end a course in writing is just a course in writing: People meet everyday. They talk about texts and structure, criticise each other, drag themselves to lunch, try to stay awake after that bowl of pasta, repeat the whole thing and then they walk home elevated by that one comment from the professor.

That dialogue is gripping!

Or like shit when a classmate feels the need to be honest.

I don't really care about psychological love dramas, can't you write about something more important, like politics?

---

[17] They usually only accepted six to eight people, every two years.

I guess when life events have a clear beginning, middle and end, we tend to label them as this one thing.

Thailand was: _____.
Studying playwriting was:_____.

It limits our capacity to actually see what has happened. How do you comprehend a whole year in a few words? I used to get really tense when people would ask me: How was Thailand? Now I get tense when people ask me: How was Berlin?
I never seem to find the right words. Where the problem is actually not the words, I have many. The problem is the question itself.
Berlin was not. Berlin still is. It's inside of me, part of my memory, my thinking, inscribed in the people I met there and as all of that is constantly changing with me, Berlin always will be and will not stop being till I stop breathing.

This will be the hardest part to write about. This is where it hurts.

There's probably a reason why so many people complain about the winter in Berlin, the layers of greyness overlapping from sky to buildings to pavements, slowly seeping into your heart. Not enough Vitamin D pills to swallow to get it out of your sight.

It's peculiar how not knowing the name of something hinders our thinking and resulting understanding of our own experience and the world around us.

Depression: I had always thought was for people that couldn't get out of bed. I was mostly angry, tired, irritated and my sleep was fine. 8 hours a night – as you can read everywhere– is the best number of sleeping hours. I was on top of my sleeping game.

The second semester had started with a pang. A short right through my fragile identity as a writer. And an email apologizing for the slight escalation of criticism that some of my colleagues had displayed upon the new play I had written over the summer break. It was called "Thailand".

That character is straight from the 1950s.

I had been the first one to show their work after not seeing each other for 2 months. It had been devastating.

I don't know. All these cliches. The ex-wife. What about feminism?

The strong female lead[18] is a category on Netflix and was at that time 2014/15 very much up and coming. Along with the term manic pixie dream girl. Which was coined in 2007 by critic Nathan Rabin in his review of the movie *Elizabethtown* to describe the quirky, optimistic flight attendant played by Kirsten Dunst. A character that "exists solely in the fevered imaginations of sensitive writer-directors to teach broodingly soulful young men to embrace life and its infinite mysteries and adventures."[19] Which fun fact: Seven years later in 2014 he regrets inventing. Because "As is often the case in conversations about gender, or race, or class, or sexuality, things get cloudy and murky really quickly. I coined the phrase to call out cultural sexism and to make it harder for male writers to posit reductive, condescending male fantasies of ideal women as realistic characters. But I looked on queasily as the phrase was increasingly accused of being sexist itself."[20]

Unfortunately there are many more of these female archetype characters if you go online and

---

[18] Definition by Wikipedia: "The strong female character is a stock character, the opposite of the damsel in distress. In the first half of the 20th century, the rise of mainstream feminism and the increased use of the concept in the later 20th century have reduced the concept to a standard item of pop culture fiction."

[19] https://film.avclub.com/the-bataan-death-march-of-whimsy-case-file-1-elizabet-1798210595

[20] https://www.salon.com/2014/07/15/im_sorry_for_coining_the_phrase_manic_pixie_dream_girl/

look for it, with analysis' that sometimes so rudimentary it is questionable whether it is actually serving any purpose. Because coining certain labels animates people to align everything under one focus, cutting off the bits that stand out. So if you want to know what I think about the whole discussion, google "strong male lead" narrative.

Oh that term doesn't really exist? It's similar to "strong main character"? Well. Fuck you Johannes! As long as that's still the case, you have to get on with the fact that I create my characters however I view reality and you will have to deal with ex-housewives in their mid-fifties, going through menopause, being incredibly mad at their ex-husbands for marrying a younger wife.

> *Who wants to hear about a housewife in her late 50s that just got divorced and exchanged for a younger version from Thailand?*

I do. Okay? I do Sebastian!

"Because what we really mean when we say we want strong female leads is: 'Give me a man but in the body of a woman I still want to see naked.'" writes the filmmaker Brit Marling in the New York Times in February, 2020.

The danger of writing schools is conformity in discourse. Which is exactly what happened. We all started writing comedy. Because the guys in our class preferred that. And yes unfortunately none of the women in my class fought against it for a while. Because the problem was not the few men, the professors, the problem was that internalised hate we had against our own themes, our own narratives. The outside world, it felt, was agreeing: Don't write female literature. Write literature. Silly, political humour, citing classics, show your intellect. Not too many feelings, please. The more absurd and abstract the better. This was after all literature and not a diary entry.

There's a poem called "How To Silence A Woman" by Dr. Clarissa Pinkola Estés I think every woman, every sensitive soul however they identify should read it:

– When they say, "You're being emotional."

Say, "Of course I have well placed emotions,

and by the way, what happened to yours?"

(…)

– When it is said, "No one wants to listen to that."

Say, "I know you have a hard time listening to

that."

Things I Have Noticed

*i feel like apocalypse now. i feel like the messiah. i feel like
you should stop reading this.* and save yourself.

2

"Why are you always looking for meaning?" The skinny guy in my bed who was supposed to be 23 but definitely looked a lot older now in broad daylight, seemed annoyed at my questioning, as I pressed my fingers on his tattoos, that looked like planets, galaxies, abstracted into symbols, circling around his arms and hands. -"I don't know. I just have to. I have to look for the truth." I said and I was quite happy about my answer, this was exactly what I would want to say, if I was in a film and this being the defining moment where the guy and the audience would fall in love with me. He was not impressed though, turned around and announced that he would go back to sleep again. Which I should, too, given the arriving comedown.

So I was this person now.

I've always had a desire for the truth, for things to be and feel real. It was hard for me to wrap my head around the fact that just 8 hours ago, I had literally thought and felt: *in love*. With this person I had just met, seen across the dance floor. I still feel a wave of cringe, when I think about how that whole evening must have looked like from the outside. 25 year old, in a fake fur coat, sitting on the tram, next to her a guy that looked exactly like someone who is dropping 4 pills a night.

Christiane F. - Wir Kinder vom Bahnhof Zoo

For a long time after that I always wondered why nobody had ever described a drug experience the way I had lived it. Before I had thought: You'd feel great, ecstatic. Things would move rapidly. Your visual would change. But mostly you would be lulled into a warm cloud. It would be a drug feeling. A special, different way of feeling.

– This is not how I felt.

I couldn't sleep so I took a shower. Scraping at the mascara bits of last night between my eyelids, my pupils still the size of black currants.
Maybe I had not been looking for the truth, but for a break. For something to be the catalyst of this shit feeling I had been carrying around for months.

It had been the first warm day after a long, dark winter. Almost like a miracle in March, the sun had shone, coats were lifted and me and one of my flatmates were drinking wine on the balcony enjoying this marvelous day that shouldn't end just yet.

Then: One of us remembered that earlier this week, she had found a bag of white powder in the belongings of another flatmate who had been on Erasmus for the past 4 months.

Minutes later: We were on our way down the stairs to find a club that was open on a Tuesday night[21].

So I was this person now.

I'm standing in a dimly lit bathroom, blood trying to pulse through my legs, crawling up slowly like a thousand ants, one hand gripping the sleek white porcelain sink, the other forming a cup, trying to get as much water inside my mouth as possible[22].

A couple of seconds later: Someone will come and hand me a coin to get free water[23] at the bar. I will make my walk across the dance floor but a bouncer will wall up before me.

---

[21] Which in Berlin is actually not that hard to find.

[22] I had heard that the biggest danger is to dehydrate when you're on drugs.

[23] The fear of dehydrating on drugs apparently nowadays can lead to over-hydrating. (mindfuck.)

I think it's better if you go home.

And I will nod and say: Yes I think so, too. I will feel relieved. Home. I can finally go home. I will be very proud of myself to still be able to get my coat at the cloak room. Finding my number in my pockets. Saying thank you and good night.
I'm on drugs but that doesn't mean I cannot be polite.

A couple of days later: I will be at Netto[24]. I will not realise that I haven't eaten anything in a long time. A shopping cart will slowly roll toward me and I will completely freak out about it. Put the few things I have in my hands on a nearby shelf and leave without buying anything.

I will read a lot about short and long-term effects[25]. About a boy in Turkey who died one week after taking ecstasy due to acute liver failure according to drugcom.de[26]. I will also freak out about that. I will talk to a lot of people about acute liver failure[27] for the next couple of weeks. And call the emergency health line because it's the weekend and I don't have a GP yet. I will be primed by the call center agent that the doctors usually do not react well toward drug-related health issues. "Do

---

[24] Which seems to be my breakdown place.

[25] Bad decision.

[26] Not sure if that's a reliable source.

[27] A real condition though.

you still want to talk to them?" and I will swallow and say: "Yes please."

5 minutes later: the doctor will ask me a question I have been asking myself for the past four days: "If you normally don't do drugs: Why did you do it then?"

I was not that person.

—

There are several voices in my head when it comes to discussing drugs. The first one is a slick, cool, sophisticated Berliner, one knee casually over the other, rolling a cigarette while she looks at me with a half smile / half smug saying something like: everybody does drugs. I only do it on the weekends. It's fine. Get over yourself. People are so stuck up about it. Yes there are risks but there's risk in everything. We will all die. Might as well have some fun. I mean, you have to be smart about it.

Then there's the intellectual, literary type that's just so annoyed by the whole topic, not another Berlin drug story, please![28] He's also really annoyed by me writing about this whole thing. He keeps saying: c'mon please. Who cares? You had a bad experience. Everybody has had a bad drug

---

[28] To quote a former professor: "Everybody thinks they are experiencing Berlin for the first time."

experience![29] So mundane. How tragic![30] He rolls his eyes a lot and doesn't allow pain to show. It might remind him of his own.

Then there's the voice probably most closest to me that thinks that: You really shouldn't do drugs. They don't make you happy. They don't make you cool. They mess with your sense of reality, your ability to feel things as they are. They're like a magnet fucking up your compass. You will not find your way home.

And then there's my mother's voice: who is just really sad about the whole thing.

That is how I explained it to my therapist. And she nodded. "That seems exhausting."

– That is exhausting.

In greek mythology there's a story, actually not one but many variations of Persephone's abduction/descent into the Underworld. Persephone is the daughter of Demeter "goddess of corn, the giver of grain and thus of bread, man's staple food, and so the great sustainer of life on earth."[31] The pair is often portrayed together with torches in their hands and crowns on their heads.

---

[29] Of course. This is not true.

[30] Asshole!

[31] From "The Penguin Book Of Classical Myths" by Jenny March.

Mother and daughter, sometimes just referred to as "The two goddesses" or "The Demeters".

There's a sacred bond between mothers and daughters.

When I was little I was afraid of a lot of things. I remember sitting on the toilet seat looking up through the skylight window above me and down to the hole, up and down, up and down, so scared that from either direction something bad could emerge. One of these nights where I would play the up and down toilet game my mother coincidentally woke up at the same time. I see her standing by the mirror, helping herself to some water. "Does it ever go away? The fear?" I ask her with all my hope for the right answer.

I'm not a mother yet, so I don't know how it feels to raise someone. I don't know what kind of fears one has to deal with. But I do know that sometimes you say things that have a major impact on someone's life without realising it. You don't know what people remember, what they blow up with meaning and keep. At that moment I doubt my mother was aware of what she was saying, but for a long time it stuck with me.

No. Quite honestly. I don't think it ever goes away.

The more widely known version of Persephone's tale is the one of an abduction:

"She [Persephone] was having a good time, along with the daughters of Okeanos, who wear their girdles slung low[32]. She was picking flowers: roses, crocus, and beautiful violets. Up and down the soft meadow. Iris blossoms too she picked, and hyacinth. And the narcissus, which was grown as a lure for the flower-faced girl by Gaia [Earth]."[33]

I was having a good time, too.

The first time I read about Persephone was deep in the midst of what I call today "the bad year" which my therapist eventually called "Adjustment disorder"[34]. I was having trouble adjusting to the current situation, which thanks captain obvious, was a diagnosis, she and I knew: was just a label, she needed to write in her little diagnosis sheet, so I could get treatment. – For a long time I was still afraid she would find something that was really really wrong with me. Beyond repair wrong.

"She [Persephone] was filled with a sense of wonder, and she reached out with both hands to take hold of the pretty flower. And the earth, full of

---

[32] Fun.

[33] From "Homeric Hymn To Demeter" translated by Gregory Nagy.

[34] Code F43. 23 is the diagnosis code used for Adjustment Disorder (AD) with Mixed Anxiety and Depressed Mood. It is sometimes known as situational depression. It occurs when an individual is unable to adjust to or cope with a particular stress or a major life event.

roads leading every which way, opened up under her. It happened on the Plain of Nysa. There it was that the Lord who receives many guests made his lunge. He was riding on a chariot drawn by immortal horses. The son of Kronos. The one known by many names. He seized her against her will, put her on his golden chariot, And drove away as she wept. She cried with a piercing voice"

Hades. God of the dead. King of the Underworld.

Like Persephone I felt like the earth had opened up beneath me and swallowed me down, way below the surface. Walking through the connecting tunnels of the Berlin underground trains, everything seemed lifeless and grey.

I don't like cities with undergrounds
people there have no foundation

The short ecstasy of a careless moment, swallowing a pill, handed to me by a stranger, downing it with a peppermint schnapps had ended in this: A mind that was leaking, falling through trap doors. Like the narcissus opening the gates to Hades.

"She [Persephone] was filled with a sense of wonder, and she reached out with both hands to take hold of the pretty flower."

But you didn't know. Did you? That the trap door would open?

For the most part of my therapy I talked about my therapy. I needed to know what was going on, what to call it and what to do about it. Very much to the annoyance of my therapist[35], it would always come up one way or another: What is my diagnosis?

In a way I thought that if we could label it, I could put it in a box and store it somewhere safe. Today I feel lucky that my therapist was never really clear about my label.

Here we're focusing on you. Individually.

As two studies that were published in 2015 in the *British Journal of Clinical Psychology* and *Behavioural & Cognitive Psychotherapy* show:
"Medical labels can be an obstacle not only to the treatment process and outcome, but can also be problematic to how the individual being labelled perceives him or herself as a person. The label is "sticky" and stigmatising, hard to remove and is unlikely to be helpful to the individual's understanding of his mental health problem."[36]

What do you gain, if I give you a diagnosis?

---

[35] I think.

[36] Quote by Dr Danny C K Lam, co-author of the two studies.

The hard part is not knowing. The hard part is realising it doesn't fit in a box, because it's everywhere. The hard part was: I was in doubt.

I would have the day off and sit on the *Ringbahn*, the train that is circling Berlin and spontaneously decide to switch trains, to drive out to Brandenburg, to a lake, skinny dip and cleanse myself from all the bullshit. And while I would sit on that train I would start to doubt my decision and feel as if it was reckless to do such a thing: A mad girl. A dramatic person that needs to do this ritual of diving into water and connecting herself to nature. I would scrutinize myself for it.

– Is that what normal people would do?

I would walk into the water, see the beauty of the sunset colouring the water in pink, purple, blue but hate myself for it. It is hard to explain this today, even to myself. But every move that I made was wrong and I would find a reason why.

Because I'm not normal anymore.

I had betrayed myself and now I was punishing myself the only way I knew how: Not trusting a single thing. My mind was leaking, falling through trap doors. Behind every thought, there was a maybe.

Maybe I was going mad now. Maybe I was not seeing things the way they are. Maybe I was going to think that I was walking through the underground like my friend who did: she thought she was sitting on the tube but actually she was in the hospital not surrounded by passengers but by patients. Her parents had finally admitted her to the psychiatric ward, when she was talking about cameras watching her every move and other conspiracy theories. Like in *The Truman show*[37].

How does that feel to think you're somewhere solid and actually be somewhere else entirely?

I was wading through Hades looking for a light while the darkness kept creeping in. I was hungry for beauty and warmth and yet I would deny myself everything.

If you eat anything from the Underworld, you'll have to stay forever.

At first Demeter does not hear her daughter Persephone's cry. But when she finally does:
"She sped off like a bird, soaring over land and sea, looking and looking. But no one was willing to tell her the truth."

Why can't you just tell me what's wrong with me?

—

[37] A film from 1998 about an insurance salesman (played by Jim Carrey) who discovers his whole life is actually a reality TV show.

The writer and Jungian psychoanalyst Dr. Clarissa Pinkola Estés whose poem I mentioned earlier writes about the Persephone myth in her book *The Creative Fire: Myths and Stories About the Cycles of Creativity*. As all characters in our dreams are a reflection of ourselves, she suggests that we also are all characters in the archetypal myths. We are Demeter – the mother, Persephone – the girl and Hades – the God of Death.

So when Persephone which in my analogy represents the naive joy, creativity, excitement, the abundance, *sanook* is captured by Hades, who is trauma and depression, after my drug experience, the pressure of art school and childhood bruises, then Demeter who was looking for her all over the land, looking for a sign to what has happened to her innocent child, that was me: going to therapy, trying to dig deep.

After my bad trip to the Suicide Circus[38], which was the club's name that me and my flatmate went to on that aforementioned Tuesday, I had been beside myself. For a while I was pretending that taking drugs was just a rite of passage of living in Berlin and talked very casually about it.

Doesn't everybody do it at some point?

I felt brave. Then I felt miserable. Because the reality of it for me was:

---

[38] You cannot make this shit up.

People with large eyes started to be terrifying. People talking about drugs started to be terrifying. Having a cold and sniffing, the feel of snot running down my throat would throw me right back into that bathroom again, talking to myself:

shit shit shit shit shit shit shit shit shit shit shit shit
shit shit shit shit shit shit shit shit shit shit shit shit
shit shit shit shit shit shit shit shit shit shit shit shit
shit shit shit shit shit shit shit shit shit shit shit shit
shit shit shit shit shit shit shit shit shit shit shit shit
shit shit shit shit shit shit shit shit shit shit shit shit
shit shit shit shit shit shit shit shit shit shit shit shit
shit shit shit shit shit shit shit shit shit shit shit shit
shit shit shit shit shit shit shit shit shit shit shit shit
shit shit shit shit shit shit shit shit shit shit shit shit
shit shit shit shit shit shit shit shit shit shit shit shit
shit shit shit shit shit shit shit shit shit shit shit shit
shit shit shit shit shit shit shit shit shit shit shit shit
shit shit shit shit shit shit shit shit shit shit shit shit
shit shit shit shit shit shit shit shit shit shit shit shit
shit shit shit shit shit shit shit shit shit shit shit shit
shit shit shit shit shit shit shit shit shit shit shit shit
shit shit shit shit shit shit shit shit shit shit shit shit
shit shit shit shit shit shit shit shit shit shit shit shit
shit shit shit shit shit shit shit shit shit shit shit shit
shit shit shit shit shit shit shit shit shit shit shit shit
shit shit shit shit shit shit shit shit shit shit shit shit
shit shit shit shit shit shit shit shit shit shit shit—

There's a live version of Nina Simone's "I wish I knew how it would feel to be free"[39], where she riffs off the last part with a new melody and improvisations. "Be transformed by the renewing of your mind" she shouts to the audience, quoting the bible. – I have been looking for that live recording for over a year now. It's not publicly available.
To me it's the most beautiful rendition of that song that I've ever heard.

"I tell you what freedom is to me: No fear." she says before the song starts to play. "If I could have that, half of my life (…) that's the closest way, that's the only way I can describe it, that's not all of it, but that's something to really feel. Like a new way of seeing, like a new way of seeing something."

I was seeing eyes too big.

Like Persephone snatched away from a moment of innocent bliss in a golden carriage, dragged down to the Underworld by Hades, I myself had been trapped in a world that felt unfamiliar and strange. I kept thinking: It didn't use to be that way. I want to get back to normal: I was determined to move on.

When Demeter finally finds out what happened to her daughter, that she was crowned Queen of the Underworld, raped by Hades, she sinks into a deep depression and the whole land turns dark and

---

[39] In the documentary "To Be Free: The Nina Simone Story"

barren. A year goes by and the gods are worried that there will be no life left on earth if Demeter does not lift her mood again.

Zeus the brother of Hades who secretly had conspired to marry off Persephone to Hades, realises he is powerless over Demeter's pain. He orders Hades to give Persephone back into the hands of her mother.

Hades obliges and sets Persephone free. But not without an evil scheme.

"He [Hadês] gave her, stealthily, the honey-sweet berry of the pomegranate to eat, peering around him. He did not want her to stay for all time over there, at the side of her honorable mother."

As Persephone eats six pomegranate seeds, from the Underworld, she is to stay half the year there. That is the pact, she unknowingly signs. Half way up, half way down. Summer and winter.

It might be that you have a shadow. Like an after-effect.

The psychiatrist told me that I was supposed to see, to check if I needed medication. The words would come slowly out of my mouth as if I was chewing on them. "Will it go away?" – "Not sure. We will run some blood tests to see if everything else is okay. You'll need to come back again in four weeks."

I hated going to the psychiatrist. He was only a couple of years older than me and seemed like someone I could meet at the Berghain.

The last time I will see him is months later, when I'll walk by a small group of protesters that are walking down Friedrichsstraße. Most of them will be dressed in white lab coats. They will be demonstrating for better work conditions and payment for psychotherapists in clinics. It will be strange to see him there, like a scene from a movie. In slow motion, a head tilted, a look, everything beyond is blurry.

At first I will not recognize him, only steps later after I will have passed him, I know it is the last time I will probably ever see him. I wish I had smiled.

You'll have to bear Damocles' sword over your head for a little while longer.

He used to say. A sword hanging by a single hair of a horse's tail over one's head. I wanted to grab it and cut myself free.

Things I Have Noticed

I need to move on. I need to be a river. Like the Amazon.
I have piranhas inside me. And crocodiles.
And things undiscovered.

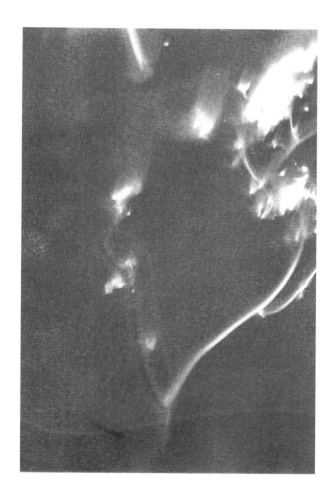

3

Sometimes the world sneaks into my backpack and weighs me down. When I was younger I would lie on my bed and feel the weight and slowly, slowly a thought would emerge, an idea. Something that would catapult me back up again, toward the sky. I would use that feeling of purposelessness, my need for meaning, it would be necessary to take me to a better place. Sometimes when I was uninspired, I would miss it, like an old friend that hasn't called for a long time and wonder where it had gone.

And then for a while I had forgotten all about it and was completely irritated when it's companion depression showed up. Immediate existential dread can be nourishing, it can be the fertilizer for creativity, a need to say something, to shout it from the top of a mountain. Depression is the opposite of that. It's slow, hard to detect in the beginning, lulling you to sleep.

I remember the moment I grasped the concept of death. I was sitting on top of the counter around eight years old and my Mother would chop tomatoes. I would ask her about the universe and where people go when they die. "We don't know." she said. And suddenly I could feel my mind expanding to the size of an endless void. The moment grown ups are honest about their limitations, is terrifying.

The following years I tried to imagine: nothingness. I would lie in my bed before falling asleep and contemplate death. I would sit in the classroom and occasionally think: What is the point? I would still function and for most of the day ignore the existential dread that was creeping in. I became quite good at it. For long stretches I would forget all about it. Sometimes I would ask my friends: Do you ever think about death? And be surprised that some of them: Never thought about it! As if you could do that. As if I simply had chosen the wrong option.

I'd like the one with the non-existential dread please. Thank you.

The year I turned thirteen was the worst. I was bullied at school, the girls bathroom became my sanctuary but I didn't tell anyone. Or maybe I did? I'm not sure I had the words for it. When the boys[40] at my school would get bullied their school bag landed in the dumpster or was thrown out of the window, they would be dragged under the shower in the locker rooms fully clothed. When girls[41] at my school would get bullied, someone would write something with a permanent marker on the bathroom walls, they would stop talking to you or spread rumours. They would use psychological warfare[42]. It's hard to show these scars. It's hard to talk about something that's so elusive. Your word against mine.

I don't remember my first panic attack but I remember going to the doctor's a lot to check up on my stomach, my heart, my bowels something was clearly wrong with me.

I also remember not knowing for quite a while what a panic attack actually was. Because I wasn't panicking. I was having a serious heart problem or something. I guess I imagined a panic attack, like someone screaming and waving their arms violently around them. You know: panic! I didn't know then that the panic would be in my head and absolutely nobody would be able to see it but I would feel like I was screaming and waving my arms violently around me, even when I was just carefully pinching my arm, to not disassociate.

[40] Gender is a construct.

[41] Gender is fluid.

[42] However the result of social norms is real.

I have friends who never in their life had a panic attack. I wonder what that feels like. I do sometimes wonder if I, as a whole, am not suitable for this environment, like fern that regularly dies in my flat. Or if something happened.

"Did something happen? I cannot help you if you don't tell me!" The young doctor is almost shouting at me, as if I have a hearing problem. He does not like it, that I'm here in the minor injury unit, shivering for no apparent reason. "Did something happen?" he asks again, a bit quieter trying a different tone. I trace the stitches from my stockings, stitch by stitch, little holes I'd like to hide in.

I'm in my first semester at Uni studying theatre and media studies at the Ruhr University Bochum. It's not Berlin, but it also starts with a B. I am yet too shy to apply for the University of Arts and pursue what I actually want to be: a writer.

So I make up my mind like a lot of people make decisions. I take whatever sounds more reasonable, sensible to others, to my parents and societal norms, so I can rationally justify my decision with the least amount of bravery and the most amount of nobody cares as long as you stay in line, though of course it clearly makes no sense to me at all.

It never does. When something isn't quite right, those shoes will always slip and eventually fall off your feet.

But I'm good at pretending.

Just right now it's getting a little harder, because I think that I'm dying. I rock back and forth on the examination table, breathing heavily.

"Did you take any drugs?" – "No." I clench my teeth. Which is true. Unfortunately I am like this without any drugs in my system.[43]

The woman in the bed next to me has stones in her gallbladder. She reminds me of my grandmother who used to dye her hair in the same colour: aubergine. It looks quite desolate, hanging from her head like sad plucked feathers. She asks me if I mind, if she smokes on the balcony. I don't. I would ask her if she could spare me one but I'm occupied with not dying. The nurse tries to give me a sedative to help me sleep but I decline. I don't need to be sedated. They just need to find out what is wrong with my body. She brings me a hot water bottle instead.

A couple of years later I will sit in a writers workshop. I will have gotten a scholarship for a novel that I'm writing. The novel will begin with that scene. A young woman in a hospital. Unable to understand what is happening to her. I will change the place to Vienna and the reason why the young woman is in the hospital will be, as we find out at the end of the novel, is because her sister had killed

---

[43] Björk doesn't do drugs either: "It [acid] just totally isolated me and I was not in touch with anyone in the room and I couldn't speak to anyone and I was in another galaxy." she said in an interview that was published 2007 in the gay magazine Attitude. She took half an acid once.

herself. Something like that. I never really could decide. But it had to be something severe. A real reason, so the reader – you – could be like: Yes, that makes sense. That's a reason to go mad.

For a long time I will call the novel: Splinters *(Splitter)* – I will not finish it.

The workshop will be attended by seven young aspiring writers, three writing school students, the headmaster of a writing course, a couple of members of the literary organisation that hosted the workshop and a delegate from the writers guild of Austria. I will be the last to get feedback that day. And then I will walk home crying. I will not cry while I sit there, with a frozen smile. We are not allowed to say anything while we get our feedback, so I don't. We are allowed to ask three questions at the end of it. I don't have any.

Every time after that day, I will open the document on my laptop and see an angry old man's face, bewildered and fuddling with the pages in front of him: "Maybe I just feel like her parents! I just don't understand what her problem is!?"

The next morning the young doctor escorts me to another room, to do some tests.

"Does it hurt here?"

- "No."

"Here?"

- "No."

I feel like I'm a bad patient. I say that my heart is racing. He tells me it's working fine. That in fact it is just doing its job. There'd be a problem if I wouldn't feel it. He is joking but I don't think it's funny.

Years later I will understand a bit more. Why my body and mind were at war at that time. I will solve a part of the puzzle. I will hold on to a line that I read a couple of years later in a german newspaper called *Die Welt*. In an interview with Madonna the journalist is quoting an old Police song: "You will see light in the darkness. You will make some sense of this."

I will.
But not now.

Things I Have Noticed

I was staring at the stuff unmoved for hours catatonic as if by possessing all these things –
I myself had become an object waiting to be thrown out.

4

The worst part is losing your voice.

All my life I saw myself as a writer. Not necessarily in a professional way but as a way of processing life. I would feel something and write it down. It had started the day my sister gave me a small red book from the penny store when I was eight years old. It had a cherry blossom tree and a woman wearing a kimono on it. I would write in that book till I was sixteen. (I was not the most consistent writer.) I had other diaries in between but this one was where I would write the important stuff e.g. I hate my {insert random family member} or my crush is xxx. A lot of pages are about me contemplating death. And whether I should move to Thailand. My diaries are surely the least happy place that I possess. But they are necessary to help me cope.

I lost my voice at some point.

It would start with lying in bed and pretending not to hear the party that my flatmate was conducting on weeknights. Or not talking in class, even though I had a lot to say. And slowly it would crawl into my hands, making me unable to write. It would frighten me to write anything down to see my thoughts, as if they could attack me once on paper. I would doubt each letter, they would only be proof that I was crazy. I would cry and deny myself any outlet. For a while I was holding it all in. Writing was dangerous. I was dangerous. It was better to keep it shut and let no one, including me, see what was going on in my mind.

Life is hard when you trust no one. It is hardest when you don't trust yourself.

"How do I know I won't go mad at some point? If a person that is suffering from an acute psychosis does not realise it, because it is inherent of the condition to not realise that you are, how on earth can I trust it is not happening right now? How can you be so sure you're not psychotic?" I asked my therapist once during a session after I had just walked passed a naked woman running down the Schönhauser Allee, breaking down on her knees praying. Her hair had been long and silky, tied in a loose knot in the middle. She had looked so clean. A couple of minutes later, the police had wrapped her in gold foil to warm her, while she was rambling words. It had not felt like a coincidence. What if I was that woman?

"We are all mad here." says the Cheshire Cat in Alice in Wonderland. "But I don't want to go among mad people," Alice remarks.

Her body like a Botticelli painting thick and ripe. Red streaks on her knees from touching ground. She makes a cross. Head to shoulders. Fingertips on pink pale skin. Gets up again. She's running from or for something. We can't tell. Shivering despair. Somebody should help her! Can somebody help her please? No tattoos, no marks or signs. She's rambling words. Spitting them on the street like graffiti tags. Nothing in particular. No colour in her long flax hair. She creates a group of witnesses. We are all entangled in this. For a moment. We all think.

What happened to you?
What the fuck has happened to you?

This is how my second novel begins. It is called Lupa. It is currently on pause, till I have written this. Till I have written all of this down, so I have no other choice but to invent something new.

There's always one question that a writer gets asked, when the protagonists is seemingly similar to the writer's persona:

Is it autobiographical?

It's a question that I would usually deny in the past. Sometimes for self-protection, sometimes cause it wasn't, sometimes for legal reasons, mostly because of vanity. There's a sense of amateurism when you write about your life and mask it with some tweaks here and there. Changing a profession to a similar one, swapping Paris for London, a boyfriend for a best friend, put in a dramatic device: someone's death / incurable sickness / a breakup / a fight, a coincidence that fits too well into the story, a change of gender.

As a writer you can create all these things when writing fiction, you can make things right. Make things make sense. Like a filter you put over the mundane colours of everyday life.

Which I guess is why through the weirdest circumstance I find myself writing non-fiction now. Because I don't want to mask it. I don't want to invent something that will seem real but won't be. It's the only way I know how to tell the truth.

So. Yes. This is autobiographical.

It took some months of therapy to realise that I had started a war against myself. "You don't seem to like yourself very much right now?" my therapist would say and weirdly enough that was news to me. Because if you would have asked me: Do you like yourself? I would have said: Yes. Of course! Who doesn't like themselves? But sometimes the automatic answer is just that: automatic and actually untrue. Like a printer telling you that there isn't enough ink in the cartridges even though you can see that there's plenty. Like machines – people – sometimes automatically lie.

I find my voice again.

When you read about famous female authors you also read a lot about suicide. Or at least that's what it seemed like to me for a while.
Another trap door: Silvia Plath. Virginia Woolf. Sarah Kane. I would look for similarities like: age, character, circumstances.

I would think: As long as I'm still writing in a cohesive way, as long as I stuck to the rules and didn't get too experimental, nothing would happen to me. I was so afraid of being perceived as weird or strange, as incomprehensible. As if madness was contagious by similarity of lifestyle and character.

I find my voice again.

I write to the psychiatrist. We have seen each other three times now, without anything happening. No prescription, just a couple of tests. I would sit there and tell him how I feel, he would tell me that I seem better each time. I would agree. Each time less afraid of his diagnosis. (I want a diagnosis but it has to be the right one.) He never mentions it. He just says: Come back again in four weeks.

Things I Have Noticed

The sword of Damocles'.

After the fourth time I write to him: I'm fine. I will not come back again in four weeks. I don't think I need medication. Therapy is working just fine. Thank you. He replies: Ok. Great[44]

I don't know what to do with my voice.

Three years after the workshop of my first never finished novel *Splitter* (Splinter), a book comes out, written by Ronja von Rönne. A german novelist a few years younger than me. It's a story about a young woman, going to therapy, suffering from panic attacks and depression and writing everything down in a notebook as her therapist advises. At the end of the story we find out that her best friend has died and she was unable to cope with her loss. I read it in one quick sip.

That's what you do with your voice.
You "say it loud. Say it clear. For the whole wide world to hear."[45]

So what happened to me?

The reason I had lost contact with myself, lost trust? – Nobody had died. Nothing that you could

---

[44] That's literally all he writes.

[45] Lyrics from "I wish I knew how it would feel to be free" Nina Simone.

put in one instance had happened. It wasn't that one time I took ecstasy and fell into a depression afterwards. It wasn't that boyfriend (not just one actually) who didn't accept my boundaries or the pressure of art school and people scrutinizing each other for validation. It wasn't Berlin with its dark corners, and concrete buildings, its mad people and homeless souls. Not sharing a room with strangers when I was a child. Not the internet. Not the bread. The gluten. The dairy. The writing on the wall in the girls bathroom. The chain-smoking and inherent hypochondria. The always black-wearing coolness of Berlin hipsters. Not my sensitive brain. Not the time my parents didn't drive to the hospital because it was the middle of the night. Or my never ending wish to please everybody. To be normal and special at the same time.

– It was not a single thing. It was all of it.

Intertwined my life had brought me to my knees. And so nothing really was a quick fix. There was not one moment that made it alright again. Not one breakthrough but many. It took time, a lot of it. And even today, sometimes I can feel the faint shadow of doubt hovering over my head. When I'm tired, exhausted, when things happen beyond my control, which let's face it, happens just fucking constantly. But having been in the darkest place I could ever imagine. I always remember this one moment between the long pauses of silence and staring at my hands, sitting in my therapist's office.

"Why can't you just tell me if I'm going to be okay?" I asked her. Tears in my eyes. My hands pressing into each other.
I just wanted her. to. tell. me. that. I. am. going. to. be. okay.
She didn't wait to think but instead almost shouted at me.

Because I want you to grow up!

How a toddler is looking for their parents after they fall to see on their faces whether they're in pain, I was still looking for others to assess the situation. A thirty year old toddler now.

When the only person I had to look for was myself. My own pain, acknowledging and deciding what to do with it.

Things I Have Noticed

part three: finding

"For an hour I am beyond desire.
It is not out of myself, but in myself.
I am."

Nan Shepherd, The Living Mountain

1

There are two things I think about when it comes to finding things.

Firstly: There's a Native American saying, that I read somewhere in a book I cannot remember or I have seen it in a film or on a TV show, that says: "Things reappear when they want to be found. Till then they are lost." I often think about that when I look for my keys, for my phone, tickets, lipsticks, passports, excuses, dreams, memories, new lovers. It gives me a certain peace of mind that I don't need to go and look for them, that there in fact is actually no point in looking, as it is not decided by me when the reunion should take place.

Secondly: There's a children's game in Germany that was played at every birthday party I went to between the ages of four and seven. One child would be blind-folded and equipped with a wooden spoon, crawl on all fours, trying to find the metal pot that had some treats hidden under it. The other children not blind-folded would shout at the top of their lungs, whether it was "cold" or "hot" increasing the degrees the closer the blind-folded child got to the pot. Finding something is just like that. Taking off your blind fold and banging that pot: Hot Hot Heat.

The summer I couldn't pay rent and went hiking instead, very much felt like that. I had just moved from Berlin to Edinburgh and was trying to get my feet back on the ground. I wasn't homeless. I had an address. I had a passport. I wasn't living on the streets. Not a social case. Not looking for pity here. I just didn't have enough money. That's all.

At first it was a joke. I didn't mean it when we were sitting in the pub, pints in front of us. It was funny. It was meant to underline the fact that I had hit a wall. That I should be looking for a job. A paid job. Money. Anything. Really. And then it became true, I think, as I'm standing in front of the white sign with black letters spelling: Coastal Path.

The rain is dripping on my neck, my dog Filou looking at me the same way I feel: miserable. It hasn't stopped raining in days. I take a picture of him and the sign for later, when I'm home again and able to pretend that somehow this moment was worth taking. That I am fine. That it was in fact fun, something you can post on instagram #nature #breath #exploringthewild. But for now I am not sure.

My shoes make squirting noises due to the fact that they are soaked with water. I guess trainers are not really appropriate footwear for hiking. I guess hiking boots would have been appropriate but also too expensive at the moment. This is going to be a cost-cutting action, I had to remind myself browsing through the shop earlier this week looking for a raincoat. Nature is free. If we could afford fancy hiking gear this would be a nice holiday trip. If we would have made better decisions in the past we would be home enjoying take-out pizza and some reality-show. But we are not. We are here. Just you and me Filou. He snorts in agreement.

The first night I sleep on a cliff. I wonder if it's dangerous, if I should know these things instinctively, if my body should tell me automatically in which direction to pitch a tent, like how it knows how to breathe. It doesn't. Not really. All I sense is: Maybe not so close to the edge.

As I lie there listening to the rain, making note of any unusual sound, Filou close by my side, I try to avoid thinking about men. Because somehow I'm really not afraid of any women entering my tent. I pet him, always repeating in my mind that he would tell me if someone was coming.

I think of the knife I brought with me. I put it beside my head. Just in case. I remember I have some wire with me too and start to tie the zippers together so the tent can't be opened from the outside. I watch the zippers for a long time as they rattle along in the wind and I start to worry about what might happen if I need to get out really quickly. If there's a fire for instance or murderers, rapists, thunder storms, being struck by lightning, rapists, rapists, rapists-murderers till finally my brain shuts down.

Nothing has happened. That's my first thought upon waking. I know the night has ended. And for that all my fear is somehow gone. As if nothing bad could ever happen in broad daylight. I untie the zippers and look at the sky. It's still quite dark but there's a glimmer of sunlight at the bottom of the horizontal line. I sit cross-legged in my sleeping bag enjoying the change of light from orange to pink to violet and blue. It is worth the fear at night, I think as I pack up. Following the coastline looking at the sea carrying wave after wave.

Wandering narrow paths gets you questioning. Blisters on both feet keep you grounded. And a phone battery that's slowly dying keeps you going. It's hard to describe what is actually happening when you're walking.

Every now and then I'm wondering about my flat, which technically isn't my flat, as I'm just renting it, which technically makes me renting it out to other people a thing that some people might call 'forbidden' or 'illegal' but I try to avoid that thought[46]. Especially now that it's already done, I try to have more constructive thoughts. Like: This is beautiful. Or. This is even more beautiful.

I notice the changes of the landscape, I try to remember the path with as much detail as possible. I try to be as present as possible, soaking in the beauty of it, but I cannot stop thinking of my own narration. How I will tell the story later. How I will say this was an enlightening experience. How I want this to be about overcoming fear, how I feel calmer the second night I lie down, but I don't.

I set up my tent right next to the rocky beach, on a small patch of grass. The beauty and secludedness of this place is beyond anything I've ever seen. I make a fire using almost half of my notebook paper but then I get anxious of the fire burning down my tent at night or attracting other wanderers so I put it out again. My fear kills all romance.

I lie awake as I try to figure out a way not to be afraid. I try to be rational about it. I try to tell myself how I don't need to be anxious before anything is even happening. That I should be anxious when I hear something or if somebody is actually presenting themselves as a threat. I repeat it over and over in my head without any resolution but eventually I pass out and again the next morning as soon as the sun rises I feel fine again.

---

[46] Edinburgh in fact is the declared capital of airbnb flats. During the Fringe, the annual Edinburgh Festival that takes place for the whole of August, prices sky rocket up to an average of: £208 per night.

I wonder, as I walk into the next village to get some breakfast, if I should just accept the fear at night as part of this journey. Like the fact that the bakery isn't open before 10 o'clock which leaves me very hungry and restless, continuing my way along the coastal path. I could have stopped, I hangrily admit to myself as I approach the national reservoir, with no food on me and miles away from any form of supermarket.

High up the top of a cliff where there's a beautiful lighthouse I sit down and watch the seagulls shrieking like my hunger. I'm angry at the other people with their light bags, just out for a stroll, for a Sunday wander. I'm sure they had plenty to eat this morning. I hate them. I hate them so much. It's not their fault, obviously it's all my fault. I start crying but nobody can hear it because the seagulls are way louder. Filou isn't even paying attention. He just wants to continue walking, pulling on the lead, so I give in.

Six hours later my mood has gone from angry to desperate. I cut through a golf course. Apparently that's not allowed or whatever but everyone is too polite to say anything. I follow the signs to the city centre. I check every five minutes on my phone which way to go, even though there is really only one street to the restaurants (plural!). Choice is too overwhelming at the moment, I just want to eat, so I collapse on the nearest seat. I wait forever (?) for the waiter to come to my table because I cannot risk any friction with him. He who has no idea why this young woman is ordering so much food but I have to make sure that there's enough and fast.

All the food arrives at once and I feel like praying. I bite into the white bread with butter, topped with tomato and basil. I dip it into the garlic olive oil sauce of the shrimps. I order more butter because it's not enough. And mayonnaise because he forgot to bring it. The fries taste hot and oily and salty and I cry. I am so happy. My phone freshly charged I get a message from the Airbnb App. Another couple is asking if they could rent the flat for next week. I make a pause and look up at the other tables; the Sunday walkers and the families with their half-eaten plates carelessly leaving them for the lingering seagulls. I look down again, click accept, get my things and leave nothing.

Beauty does not need to have a point.
It just is.

2

As with most myths from centuries ago, there are usually several versions existing. The pre-hellenic version of the Persephone myth is profoundly different from the one I re-told in part two. Here it is not Hades who abducts Persephone, dragging her into the Underworld. It is herself who is choosing to go.

One day Persephone finds herself playing in the meadows as she hears through a crack in the soil the voices of people crying, desperately, hopeless. Wondering why the voices are so miserable and moved by deep compassion, she descends to the Underworld. Finding lost souls wandering beneath the earth and affected by their sorrow she decides to help them and guide them into the world beyond the living. "There was a need for this work that remained unfulfilled, and Persephone chose the path of courage, diving head first into the role she was destined to play."[47]

---

[47] https://www.astrologywithheather.com/goddess-insight/2016/11/1/the-goddess-persephone-a-mythological-breakdown

This is an interesting shift from the patriarchal violence portrayed in the first version. Here Persephone willingly descends into the underworld, curious and brave, trying to help, to nurture whoever is in need of a helping hand. Guiding them. Death being part of the cycle of life. Knowing: There's no such thing as an eternal summer. That we must face our darkness.

I was 18 when I visited Edinburgh for the first time. I stepped out of the train station and it was pouring down. Little streams flowing down the streets. The air humid, like a cloud hugging me. I fell in love immediately. Walking up Cockburn Street, the pebbles glistening in the grey light, the narrow steps up the Advocates Close, like stepping into a gothic dream.

Stranding on the royal mile, a bagpipe playing nearby, my steps taking me down the street and up left Calton Hill, overlooking the city, sea in the north, Arthurs Seat towering in the east. I didn't know any of the names of these places yet, I wouldn't know them for my stay there but something would leave me that day, a promise silently uttered to the ground.

11 years later I am standing at the exact same spot on Calton Hill, surrounded by the ocean and countless rooftops. It's a good place to make a decision. Hills regularly are. I am standing next to my younger self. Looking at her, the things she feels, the things she doesn't know yet. The things she

knows and I forgot. Memories, wishes, promises, regrets pile up between us.

I ask myself if I should stay here. It's been three months since I stepped from that ferry in Newcastle: In front of me a calm ocean blue. The sun rising some feet above. It's beautiful as it's banal: The sun also rises again and again. The sound of the waves and the engines merging into a symphony. Breathing in deep deep with a pinch of salt. I'm in transit. Somewhere between Amsterdam and Newcastle. Alone on deck. My thoughts stretch wide. Maybe I will find a home in Edinburgh? Maybe I will stay forever? Later that morning we'll sit here again and have scones with clotted cream, lemon curd and my friend J smiling at me, smiling at the sea. Talking about how the best way to travel to Scotland really is by ship. And I think that is all the more true an hour later when we sail into the bay. Two lighthouses guarding it on each site. „Mouth of the Tyne". Swallowing us, our hopes, our tired excited bodies.

The first days I spent a lot of time wandering around Stockbridge[48], enjoying my new neighborhood, the Water of Leith walkway close by, the view from Inverleith Park, the botanical garden. I make friends at a bookclub and think of this

---

[48] Stockbridge has something of a village atmosphere about it, although it is only a ten to fifteen minute walk from Edinburgh city centre, it is quite secluded with its own Sunday Market, the Water of Leith path and cute cafes and shops.

saying that you're home in a city once you made a friend there. I plan to make many.

I sit in cafés reading magazines and eating Battenberg cake. I find the poetry library and fall in love with Edinburgh all over again. „If I could invent a place, it would look like this." I tell my friends in Berlin and I mean it.

I look for a job in a café and I get it. I make more friends. I go hiking in the Pentlands. Climbing over fences on Midsummer to get lucky. I only wish for one thing, as I watch the sun ascend over the hills in the early hours of morning wrapped in my tartan blanket. Love. I always wish for love. I always look for it. I go swimming in the sea, collect sea shells and more wishes.

I walk through all of these new and old memories as I stand there on Calton Hill. As it all becomes so clear, I can touch it with my bare hands.

Edinburgh - The magical city where everything intertwines. I cannot explain it but something draws me here like a call from the past, a memory, a path I just have to take. There's something hidden. I can feel it in my bones. I scatter them all over the city trying to resurrect something from the dead, the unknown world. Like Persephone ascending, initiating spring. Trying to resurrect myself.

~~This is about a soufflé.~~
This is about survival.

3

I have never made a soufflé. I don't even know what it should taste like but as everyone who grew up with a TV since the early 1950's knows: Soufflés are the highest culinary accomplishments on this planet. Quite impossible to master and almost always done by people who are especially incapable to undertake such an endeavor. Being at a particular low point of my life, my job recently lost, a looming pandemic and rejection after rejection flooding my email folder, I as it appears am a perfect candidate: And should I win. And it would rise. So should I.

I cannot tell you where the idea actually came from. Soufflé jokes are certainly a dead TV trope and anyone trying to use any sort of pun that uses „deflating" is offensively unoriginal. These jokes belong to our Dads, they shall keep them. But somehow the thought crossed my mind on a particularly bad and unsuccessful day as I was leaving the kitchen walking into my room devouring yet another snack. One of the routines I had perfected during the lockdown[19].

Was it the emptiness of a 5 o'clock sugar-low? Or my self-esteem that was craving any form of validation, by gaining a sort of control over my life, mastering something so extremely difficult? Or was it the premise of the movie Julie & Julia that I had re-watched during one of those long lockdown-days where one skims through the what-to-watch history and then ends up with something they have already seen. Amy Adams who plays an unhappy writer (me?) unfulfilled in her career (me?) decides to do something good for herself (me!) by cooking all the recipes from Julia Child's cookbook „Mastering the Art of French Cooking".

– Either way somehow weeks later all those scenes of soufflés gone wrong came rushing through my head as I stood in the hallway stopping in motion, snack mid air: Actresses playing desperate housewives urging guests not to speak too loud or make any form of sudden movement, because we

---

[19] The first one. Funny how back then it was just "the lockdown".

all know soufflés are highly sensitive to sound,
motion, air, intrusive thoughts. Soufflés poofing,
exploding, collapsing, terrorising. The fear. The
angst. The labour. I started my research at once.

The first recipe of a soufflé was published in the
1814 cook book by Antoine Beauvilliers "The Art
of French Cookery" who apparently was cooking
for the upper class including royalty like Madame
Pompadour[50]. French star cook Eric Lanard
apparently created an orange soufflé in her honor, a
soufflé literally rising out of an orange. Extravagant
like her, something to try out later I noted, when
glamour would enter my life again[51].

Diving deep into a forum titled *What happened to
soufflé humour?* I felt solace in the comments such as:
„I'm 21, and I've never actually seen one in real life,
just on TV or in movies." or „I feel like even in the
90s, soufflé jokes were all from writers' 20-year-old
childhood memories of soufflés in the 70s, and no
one had actually eaten a soufflé in like a decade." or
„People don't cook soufflé anymore because they
think they are a hassle. The cartoons did too good a
job brainwashing people!" Reading them a soufflé
could very well be the invention of film and TV

---

[50] One of these famous names where one has a vague inclination of
what they entail but has in fact no idea who these people actually were.
Madame Pompadour like an onomatopoeia, a word that sounds like
the thing it is describing, extravagant, voluptuous, pomp, was the chief
mistress of Louis XV, I find out googling. From what I understood of
her biography would be called nowadays "state secretary with
benefits".

[51] Still hasn't.

writers, imagining the perfect dish to illustrate the inner turmoil of their characters. Billy Wilder's movie classic *Sabrina* for instance: A young Audrey Hepburn plays an "ugly duckling" and transforms into a beautiful swan by going to France and learning the hard to obtain french cuisine and chopping off her hair. Also known as the mother of soufflé scenes: "Too low; too high; too heavy; sloppy" the stereotypical french chef is commenting one soufflé after the other ending with Sabrina's and declaring that the emotional state of a woman is transparent while baking: "A woman happy in love, she burns the soufflé. A woman unhappy in love she forgets to turn on the oven." I wondered what happened to women who lost their job and were trying to put their life back together?

Choosing a recipe how I have chosen all of them in the past by taking the first one that pops up with a promising photo, looking at the author, I felt it was a sign: Mary Berry from *The Great British Bake Off* would be my guide. Also because Mary promised if I followed all the instructions carefully I would get "great results." I was determined to do that. I was determined to really read the whole recipe beforehand and make sure I did so twice. Unlike my usual procedure: Skim the recipe, buy most of them, hope for the best. This time I would: Buy the exact ingredients, make no exceptions and also hope for the best. I would excel at this. If I could do this, I could do anything.

I could survive this pandemic, the soufflé would be my proof. I could get a job again. I could forget about that brazen email my former boss had sent out to all of us. I could forget about it all.

I am very disappointed. That you should think we abandoned our weekly paid staff.

"You have to butter the ramekins" was Mary Berry's first order. Ramekins, which I realised I hadn't really thought about getting. Technically not an ingredient I assured myself. Glass ramekins leftover from store-bought cheesecakes would have to make do. I was picturing them for a moment bursting in the oven, not resisting the heat, glass splinters everywhere but I would take that risk. I felt 80% sure it wouldn't happen.

The next step was to coat them with a thin layer of sugar and then chill them in the fridge. Following instructions, knowing right from wrong. It gave me a sense of order and purpose again. Following a recipe does that to you. I already felt better about myself. Which is probably why I sometimes feel like rebelling against it. Because sometimes you don't want order and beauty, sometimes you want chaos and change.

– It had been in the first week of lockdown. Sent home with the words: "You don't need to come again tomorrow." We all had left the premise with a sense of confusion and despair. I had lunged down in a squat pose for a minute to collect myself, one of my superiors commenting it with: "You shouldn't attempt such a dramatic pose". In hindsight a bleak statement. A couple of days later we were informed that we would be paid for the rest of the month but then no longer. It had been a single sentence in an otherwise very lengthy email describing the company's survival scheme in these „unprecedented times". As if it was insignificant. A minor information, only for those with a zero-hour-contract. As if by saying: You're earning so little. How can you miss it?

That you should think we abandoned our weekly paid staff.

The other employees with – to put it bluntly – „real contracts" would still be paid during the lockdown. I proved to be exactly what my father had always warned me: A person with no safety-net. – It was not then when I snapped.

Soufflé comes from the french word *soufflér* meaning breath; a breath constituted of exact timing and transitory at its core. A breath of fresh air was what I desperately needed now, as breathing had become difficult over the past weeks. Anxiety and panic had found their way in again. Depression my old pal had paid a visit and as all uninvited guests had not mentioned a departure date yet. He was waiting for me on the couch, wrapping blankets around me, telling me I don't need to take a shower or brush my teeth or for that matter do anything really instead of lie down, rest and give up.

Which I did for a while, until another email from my former employer entered my inbox.

I am very disappointed.

I guess it was well intended. Trying to bring a little life into the first weeks of lockdown distress. It spoke about the achievement of the company, how everyone was chipping in and supporting each other, photos of cute pets and recommendations on what to watch this week. It even had a few jokes about the upper managers now finally having time to play golf.[52]

No words of comfort for the people with no income prospects, no apology, no explanation.

– That's when I snapped.

Jumping up from the couch, my face melting into Edvard Munch's *Scream* I needed to do something, something big and glorious. I needed to let them know that while they comfortably sat on their furloughed asses, other people did not know how to make next month's rent or food and were possibly not thinking about working on their handicap. It had to start now. It had to start with me.

It was also when I realised that the contract that I had signed was worth nothing: A standard zero-

[52] Fun?

hour-contract. Meaning, there might as well never have been a contract at all. They didn't owe me anything. I had shown up to my shifts and wiggled my plans around so it could fit the company's schedule. I had promised my labour to them but only as long as they needed it. Pandemics not included. I had lived in an illusion of a regular employment-ship, of being part of a team. Now it was time to step out of it. Time to be my own boss.

That you should think we abandoned our weekly paid staff.

At least that's what I told myself writing that email. It had felt good to get everything off my chest. To tell them what it felt like to go into a pandemic with no savings, no security. Someone needed to let them know that we were a vital part of the company, too. And apparently it was me.
If I ever needed to be German, that was my moment. British politeness would not do.

After I had sent it I ran along the canal near my house, all my energy that had disappeared the weeks before had magically come back. Speaking up had set *me* free. And it would definitely piss *them* off, to misquote Gloria Steinem a little bit. The air felt vibrant, every mile I left behind me, was shedding another layer. It didn't matter what they would answer. I didn't care. They knew now. That was what mattered. They saw us now. The only way was to punch up.

I do often wonder what would have happened without the pandemic. If I would have just stayed at that job, dreaming of finishing a novel I had been writing on for years, but like so many other novelists never really accomplishing it, because the constant need to provide for basic living needs was occupying all headspace and only leave enough to pretend that all this was just a temporary blip. A little pause for better prospects in the future. Surely I never would have tried to make that soufflé.

I never would have parted the egg from the yolk so meticulously. Slowly mixing the batter, folding the fluffy egg whites in as carefully as putting on a newborn's diapers.

"To become a writer I had to learn to interrupt, to speak up, to speak a little louder, and then louder, and then to just speak in my own voice which is not loud at all." writes Deborah Levy in her memoir "Things I don't want to know". Writing that email had reminded me of that. Of me. Of who I was. Who I am.

"I'm very disappointed" the answer sent to me a couple of days later from my former boss had begun. "That you should think we abandoned our weekly paid staff."

– I laughed when I read this. The audacity. The gaslighting. Of course they would not have apologised. But at least they had offered to apply for the government furlough scheme for us, if it were applicable[53]. Which meant we could get by during the turbulent months to come.

That was all that counted. I had stood up for myself and for others. I had spoken up. Closing the oven door I waited in anticipation. Through the glass I watched the soufflé.

Slowly
but surely,
catching my breath.

---

[53] It was.

Things I Have Noticed

Sophia Hembeck is a writer based in Edinburgh. Originally from Germany she is writing in English and German. She has studied playwriting at the University of Arts in Berlin and has published two graphic novels in German: This Feeling of Emptiness (2018) and Januar (2019). Several essays have appeared in Almost 30 Magazine, Dear Damsels and Severine Lit. She has a weekly Sunday newsletter called *The Muse Letter*, where she publishes essays, notes and interviews with other creatives and artists.

Find the latest on:
www.sophiahembeck.com
www.themuseletter.substack.com

Instagram: @sophiahembeck

Thank you

The initial   printing of this book was funded via Kickstarter by the loveliest and most supportive group of people a writer could hope for.

To each one of you: I see you. And thank you for seeing me.

I also need to give huge thanks to my parents, who have been supportive of me all my life, who have inspired me in many ways they don't even know. And who are mostly responsible for shipping my books in the past years, maybe even the one you are holding in your hands right now.

To Becca, who proof-read this book even though she wanted to only read it, when it's really finished and printed. (Sorry!) Thank you for having my back, always!

To Ilona for listening and Julius for being the first one to read this.

And lastly to all my dear friends, readers of the Muse Letter and people on the internet, that have taken an interest in what I do.

Things I Have Noticed

I hope you feel less alone now. I really hope you do.

Things I Have Noticed

Muse Letter Publishing
Edinburgh, 2020

Things I Have Noticed by Sophia Hembeck
Copyright 2020 by Sophia Hembeck

ISBN 978-1-5272-8041-0

Typeset in Baskerville

Printed and bound by WirmachenDruck, Germany

Look out for love, always.